My Thirty-Five Years
with
Ataxia

Hereditary Ataxia

My Thirty-Five Years with Ataxia

Hereditary Ataxia

By

Patricia Birdsong Hamilton
McDonough, Georgia

iUniverse, Inc.
New York   Bloomington

My Thirty-Five Years with Ataxia

iUniverse books may be ordered through booksellers or by contacting:

iUniverse
1663 Liberty Drive
Bloomington, IN 47403
www.iuniverse.com
1-800-Authors (1-800-288-4677)

ISBN: 978-1-4401-0842-6 (pbk)
ISBN: 978-1-4401-0843-3 (ebk)

Printed in the United States of America

iUniverse rev. date: 2/19/2009

Dedication

This book is dedicated to my family, to my husband Ed, and our children, Julnelle and Edwin, Jr.

A special thank you goes out to Richard and Maxyne Bursky, and Paul and Ruth Koku.

This book is also dedicated to "ataxians" everywhere.

"For I will restore health to you and heal you of your wounds, says the Lord." -- Jeremiah 30:17

Introduction

The manuscript of my first book, A Balancing Act: Living with Spinal Cerebellar Ataxia, was rejected by large publishers who told me that my target market was too small. Recognizing the desperate need for practical, useful information by people afflicted with this disease, I decided this topic was too important to abandon, and I went the route of working through a small, independent publisher.

A Balancing Act described my early life as a healthy, happy child; my experiences as a young adult with the beginning symptoms of ataxia; my neurological evaluation; and how the disease has affected my life.

Spinal cerebellar ataxia, also known in the medical community as spinocerebellar ataxia or SCA, is a rare, debilitating disease that I inherited from my father and grandfather. A diagnosis was made for me in 1988 at the Mayo Clinic. Suffering from advanced symptoms of the disease that made it impossible for me to continue my professional career as a financial analyst at IBM Corporation, I had no choice but to retire early and apply to the Social Security Administration for disabled status.

As a result, I suddenly found myself with lots of time to search for practical information and guidance in coping with SCA. I scoured libraries and bookstores with no luck. I discovered there was nothing available of a non-technical, non-scientific nature to help me deal with my difficulties.

In 1992, I resolved that I would document my everyday experiences and adjustments to aid others who found themselves in similar situations.

In February 1997, I took the finished product to the National Ataxia Foundation's annual membership meeting in Jackson, Mississippi. An overwhelming number of the 300 members of the organization greeted my efforts with surprise and gratitude. I was delighted to watch the supply of my copies of the book dwindle as NAF members snatched the book off the table. I knew then that I needed to continue to write within this venue in order to let others similarly situated know they are not alone

On February 14, 2005, my husband and I moved to the Atlanta, Georgia area, and on November 27, 2006, I was examined by Dr. George R. Wilmot, Neurologist, in the Neurology Center of the Emory Clinic, Emory University. It was comforting having a doctor who could pronounce and spell the word "ataxia" (a-tak-se-a).

On March 3, 2007, I took a blood test to determine the type of ataxia I have. I was diagnosed as having SCA2.

It helps tremendously for people with SCA to know that there are others like themselves going through life-altering hardships like theirs. In the words of one grateful reader of my first book, "Someone else knows my pain, and understands."

I will continue to provide practical information that will help those who for so long have felt abandoned by and isolated from a medical community that is still learning how spinal cerebellar ataxia affects individuals.

This book is written chronologically, from when my ataxic symptoms first began to manifest themselves, to the present. I discuss ideas that I have found help me cope with my medical conditions.

I am convinced that the best way to learn about ataxia is from a person who has ataxia, so I decided to write about my experiences with the disease from the layman's perspective.

Here's the way I see it: I had an old car. My mechanic worked on the car to keep it running as best he could. Nevertheless, I'm the one who had to drive the car every day. I know best how to jiggle this knob or that handle in order to get from here to there. The car may not have been in tiptop shape, but I know how to get myself where I need to go.

I have written several books and papers relating to ataxia. For a list of my current publications, see http://www.livingwithataxia.com. You may also contact me at Ataxiabooks@aol.com.

Contents

"I will restore health to you and heal you of your wounds, says the Lord."
Jeremiah 30:17

Chapter 1
What Is Ataxia?

Ataxia can be defined as follows:

❖ A debilitating disease of the central nervous system

❖ The gradually increasing loss of coordination of functions such as walking, eye movement, speech (dysarthria), improper movement of arms and legs, inability to write, etc.

❖ Hereditary or sporadic, the common hereditary types being Friedreich's ataxia (FA) and Spinocerebellar ataxia (SCA)

The spinal cord is connected to the brain; and the cerebellum, which controls coordination of voluntary motor movement, balance and equilibrium, is located just above the brain stem and toward the back of the brain. Dysfunction of the cerebellum sends mixed and incorrect messages throughout the body.

Sporadic ataxia refers to a person who exhibits ataxic behavior due to medication or due to an environmental circumstance. In this case, sporadic ataxia is itself referred to as a symptom in the medical community.

Each person's makeup is different. Therefore, one should be careful in using medication, vitamins, or herbal extracts that have not been prescribed or reviewed by a physician.

"I can do all things through Christ which strengthens me."
Philippians 4:13

Chapter 2
Ataxia Challenges Through the Years

My experiences with ataxia cover thirty-five years. I have been able to isolate at least twenty-five separate symptoms that affect me. I will describe each of them. For ease of management, I have divided the total number of years living with ataxia by three, so that each section contains approximately twelve years.

The symptoms are listed as they first occurred. All of my symptoms are discussed in chronological order.

These challenges are categorized as follows:

❖ The Onset of Ataxia Symptoms, 1973 -- 1984

❖ Symptoms Continue, 1985-1996

❖ Advancing Symptoms, 1997-2008

I detail milestones in these sections, relating each important experience with the date it first impacted my life, for example, when I had to stop driving.

The Onset of Ataxia Symptoms

o 1973 Misjudged tennis racquet swing and speed of the ball, missing the serve

o 1977 Misjudged distance and speed of a fly ball in a softball game and missed the catch

o 1979 Misjudged doorway and walked into the frame

o 1979 Suddenly slid off a chair

o 1979 Finger jerked while attempting to dial telephone

o 1980 Experienced severe and frequent muscle cramps

o 1980 Frequent loss of balance; clumsiness

o 1980 Slurred speech

It should be noted that many of these challenges preceded my formal diagnosis of spinal cerebellar ataxia. Being extremely athletic from childhood into early adulthood, I puzzled over the problems I had playing sports, as well as elsewhere in my life. As I was not formally diagnosed with ataxia until 1987, I struggled with many unanswered questions about my coordination difficulties for many years.

Some of these difficulties are due in large part to the fact that many of the symptoms I was experiencing mimicked the recognized signs of other diseases such as multiple sclerosis (MS) or Parkinson's Disease. Ataxia is sometimes misdiagnosed at first by even the best of neurological specialists. An overwhelming number of people afflicted with ataxia, whose family members had not previously been stricken with the disease, endure years of misdiagnosis.

<u>Misjudged a tennis racquet swing and speed of ball.</u> I had difficulty judging the speed and distance between the

airborne ball and contact with the racquet. I missed easy shots. I never won a game.

Misjudged a fly ball in softball. As a little girl playing with my brothers, it was apparent that I excelled at throwing and catching both a softball and a baseball. I loved to play first base, but was put in the outfield because first base was key to keeping the other team from getting on base and eventually scoring. Even easy fly balls in the outfield eluded me. I felt as if I had been banished from team play, and that sports had been stolen from me.

Sliding off a chair. Once when I was visiting a friend, I went to sit in a chair. My brain misjudged the position of the chair and ordered my body to sit down a few inches away from the target seat, and I fell on the floor. Unnoticed by my host, I quickly picked myself up, got in the chair, and pretended nothing had happened.

Misjudging doorways. It was not uncommon for me to hit my left shoulder on a door frame when leaving a room. I ran into doorways so often, I became used to the pain. It got to where I became virtually numb, and didn't even stop to consider how hurt I was.

Finger jerked when dialing a telephone. Working in a conference room with my fellow staff members and my manager, I was in the process of making an urgent and important phone call to lock in a price at a specific time. Because my finger jerked, I misdialed the number the first time and had to place the call again. Those few seconds caused our department to miss our targeted price. I felt at that moment as if everyone in my department was staring at me. I wanted to crawl into a hole. I would have done almost anything to have avoided the disappointed look on my manager's face. I was confused and upset, having no idea why this extremity had let me down – again. Needless to say, I was devastated.

Muscle cramps. This symptom can best be described as a muscle that is spastic or tight. Cramping can occur in any muscle in the body. I have experienced this discomfort in my hands, chest, arms, thighs, legs, and feet. Muscle cramps can be caused by many things, such as not enough water or the lack of it altogether for a period of time; cold temperatures; the lack of potassium; and injury.

Relief generally occurs if I do certain things specific to where the discomfort is felt. If my arms are cramping, I put on a jacket or sweater. I most often cover my hands, thighs, legs and feet with a blanket, and that seems to relieve the pain. If the pain is in my chest, I take a muscle relaxer such as calcium, or a quinine tablet. If the pain becomes extreme, I immediately contact my doctor.

Loss of balance; clumsiness. Ataxia renders a person unable to control their movements. This inability results in a loss of balance. Some medical professionals refer to this symptom as walking with a wide and/or unsteady gait.

It may be hard for someone not afflicted with this disease to appreciate the role that balance plays in doing so many everyday tasks, and how much that ability is missed when the ataxic brain misfires.

Walking; carrying a cup of tea or coffee without spilling it; bike riding; dancing; standing without leaning against the wall, sink, stove or other stationary object; putting on clothes; sitting on or getting up from the toilet; turning over in and/or getting in and out of bed; taking a shower or bath; standing and paying the grocery bill at the supermarket; these are all enormous tasks for a balance-challenged individual, ones which are taken for granted by the general population.

My first experiences with ataxia were bouts of clumsiness such as stumbling, and having little control over where I wanted my hands and arms to go. Sometimes, not meaning to exert as much force as I did, I would open a door, nearly taking it off its hinges.

I especially remember moving awkwardly up and down steps, something that was not only uncomfortable, but also dangerous. At first, I brushed off these incidents as insignificant, a glitch in my system, so to speak. But I learned differently as time passed.

<u>Slurred speech.</u> In April 1991, I began taking speech therapy. I knew slurred speech was a symptom of ataxia, and I wanted to improve my speaking skills before the problems really started. I didn't realize that they already *had* started.

I first recognized my speech was slurred when I returned home from the first speech therapy session at the Rehabilitation Center in White Plains, New York. I listened to the answering machine. I had forgotten that I left a message for my husband.

I heard a strange, unfamiliar voice. It was harsh and raspy. I could not believe it was me. My voice was totally unlike what I knew it to have been. It had radically changed.

My speech is sometimes hard to understand and I have no control over the volume. I concentrate very hard on what I am saying in order to enunciate as clearly as I can manage, but I am not always as successful as I would like to be.

The most difficult experiences I have had with regard

to my speaking efforts all relate to noticing people's reactions. There is the assumption others make that slurred speech is an indication that my mental capabilities are less than normal. Sometimes I would be completely ignored as someone turned to my husband or friend for an answer to a question that should ordinarily have been directed to me. One of the most aggravating habits people sometimes have is talking about me as if I weren't there: "Does she know what she wants to eat?" asks the ignorant waitress.

Although my slurred speech initially shocked me and fell harshly on my ears, my philosophy has been, and remains to this day, that I will never stop talking. I will never stop verbally expressing myself. I have a right to talk. After all, through the grace of God, I still have the blessing of speech, and I'm going to use it!

Symptoms Continue

o 1991 – Rapid heartbeat (Dr. Byron Thomas' office – anxiety attack)

o October 1995 – Started using cane

o November 5, 1995 – Fall in kitchen

o May 24, 1996 – Clumsiness

o June 6, 1996 – Fainted

o August 1, 1996 – Weak thighs

o 1996 – Speech slurred; fatigue; difficulty picking up coins or buttoning a blouse or shirt

1991 – Rapid heartbeat

I was new to my community and it was my first time seeing a doctor there. I had recently started trying to find reading materials on ataxia when suddenly my heart started beating fast. The doctor's examination revealed no abnormalities.

October 1995 – Started using cane
November 5, 1995 – Fall

Falling seems to be a generally common symptom with ataxia. I usually fall backwards.

In an effort to avoid falling, you should keep your walking area clear of obstacles. Pick up soap or a shampoo bottle in the shower only when holding on to a handicap bar. You can avoid falling by lightly holding onto something in the bathroom such as the sink. The kitchen sink, refrigerator, or stove edge can also serve to stop a fall.

You should also teach yourself the proper and safest way to fall. Unfortunately, it's hard to remember the procedure when you are in the process of falling. You should actually practice falling safely. You will have a much better chance of successfully recovering from a fall without injury. Falling can be managed. For example, when I lived in Florida, I had a fear of falling backward into the inground pool. In my mind, I envisioned falling into the water and taking the appropriate steps to avoid harm to myself in that event. After a time, I could walk, self-assured, on my patio, knowing what to do in case of emergency.

June 6, 1996 – Fainted

My body overheated unusually quickly after sitting in the steam room and sauna.

August 1, 1996 – Weak thighs

I could feel my thighs getting weak whether I was in a seated or standing position.

1996 – Fatigue

One cause of fatigue is the loss of energy. Therefore, I do several things to conserve energy. The most important thing is to rest and not over-exert myself. I try to take long naps, and especially make sure I nap prior to going to any event.

Avoid rushing; take your time. Do things in moderation.

Exercise is essential. Make time to exercise, of course in moderation.

Serve meals in easy-to-handle plates; and eat out as often as possible.

1996 – Difficulty picking up coins or buttoning a blouse or shirt

I experienced loss of dexterity as well as the lack of coordination in my fingers.

Advancing Symptoms (1997-2008)

o <u>April 1998</u> – Loss of balance (walking); still able to walk fast, run, and drive a car

o <u>August 25, 1998</u> – Diarrhea. Once when I was treated for heartburn discomfort, my doctor prescribed medication that was too strong; fall

o <u>August 30, 1998</u> – Left hand (fingertips) went numb while sitting on the side of the bed rolling my hair; sick to stomach, no appetite, recovered by lying down

o <u>September 1, 1998</u> – Mild chest pains; tried to relax by taking several deep breaths and resting

o <u>October 27, 1998</u> – Walking off-balance; handwriting getting worse; fell backward in kitchen

o <u>January 1999</u> – Chest pains. I usually would sweat at night; uncomfortable feeling. I would often get up and take a shower

o <u>May 4, 1999</u> – Anxiety attack; severe muscle cramps in both legs. My shin muscles in both legs, and both of my feet started hurting worse than ever before. None of the remedies used before worked this time. I would usually cover my legs with a blanket or put on a pair of socks and take medication in pill form. This time my husband took me to the emergency room where they administered medication through an IV.

o <u>October 1999</u> – Fatigue

o <u>January 2000</u> – Used shopping cart as mobility aid; stopped driving. On two separate occasions, I temporarily lost focus on my driving. Once, I was backing out of my driveway and temporarily forgot how to control the car. Once when I was driving with my son, he decided he wanted a hamburger from Burger King. After pulling out of Burger King's parking lot, I turned right, toward a major intersection, and seeing a red light, forgot how to apply the brake and stop the car.

o <u>May 27, 2000</u> – Severe dizziness. I remember the incident well. My body became limp. I was like a rag doll. I had no control of my body. My husband took me to the shower, turned it on, and sat me down in my shower chair. As the water gently cascaded down my back, I quickly felt better, and life began to come back into my body. The entire episode lasted less than a few minutes. It has never happened again.

o <u>January 2002</u> – Wax buildup in left ear. The wax that built up affected my ability to hear. I contacted an ear, nose and throat doctor, who used a rod to clean my ear. It was very painful. I thankfully have since found another doctor to do this less painfully.

o <u>January 2005</u> – Coughing/swallowing difficulty. A person usually will cough in an attempt to clear one's throat. Coughing uncontrollably is very intense, not to mention annoying. It can last from ten to fifteen minutes. The following recommendations may help:

> o Chew food slowly and thoroughly
> o Eat steamed or well-cooked foods
> o Eat small portions of food at a time
> o Drink beverages slowly through a straw
> o Eat soft foods (mashed potatoes, oatmeal, applesauce)

- o Try not to swallow too much saliva at once
- o In addition, avoid eating the following:
  - Raw foods, especially raw vegetables
  - Fish that has bones in it
  - Food that is hard to chew or swallow
  - Large chunks of meat, such as steak
  - Popcorn and unpopped kernels
  - Broccoli florets
  - Thick beverages, such as milkshakes
  - Sweets

o <u>May 2006</u> – HealthSouth Physical Therapy

o <u>June 2006</u> – Head and hands tremors. Tremor refers to shaking that is the result of a neurological malfunction. My head tremors seem to be mild, yet they are very annoying. I attempt to minimize the shaking by resting my head against the back of my sofa. My head shakes more when I am tired or tense. I concentrate on relaxing to slow down or stop the tremors when they occur in different parts of my body. Going to bed relaxes me. A trick I use to calm my body is to take deep breaths.

o <u>October 26, 2006</u> – HealthSouth Physical Therapy

o <u>November 27, 2006</u> – Exam by Dr. George Wilmot, MD – Neurologist specializing in ataxia

o <u>January 16, 2007</u> – Swallowing test

o <u>March 3, 2007</u> – Blood test for SCA2 per Dr. Wilmot. Upon moving to Atlanta, I was examined by an ataxia specialist. I was recently diagnosed with SCA2.

o <u>March 13, 2007</u> – Fall; occasional muscle cramps; continued slurred speech and loss of balance. These symptoms were experienced during all three periods and have worsened since their 1980 onset.

o <u>March 20, 2007</u> – Urination urgency. Despite surgical removal of a large, non-cancerous, water-filled growth from my stomach, I continue to have to urinate with sudden urgency.

o <u>April 3, 2007 to May 15, 2007</u> – Gentiva Home Care

o <u>December 4, 2007</u> – Extreme difficulty in walking; purchased electric and manual wheelchairs – not yet being used

o <u>August 2008</u> – Stiffness all over. In the morning, muscles, especially in legs and arms, are stiff.

o <u>September 2, 2008</u> – Fall

o <u>September 3, 2008</u> – Fall

o <u>September 23, 2008</u> – Fall in bedroom; took third MRI

"And the grace of our Lord was exceeding abundant with faith and love which is in Christ Jesus. This is a faithful saying, and worthy of all acceptation, that Christ Jesus came into the world to save sinners, of whom I am chief."
Timothy 1:14 - 15

Chapter 3
They Keep on Coming

Over the past several years, many challenges that I just want to get rid of have appeared in my life. The three most daunting and adverse to my attempts to lead a normal existence are the loss of balance, slurred speech, and tremors.

Loss of balance encompasses more than just having difficulty walking. It involves being unable to shower without holding onto a handicap bar or leaning on the shower wall; difficulty putting on clothes; trouble walking with a cup of tea or coffee without spilling it.

My voice has changed quite a bit over the years. It sounds more raspy. Another difference in my present voice from the past that I have learned to accept is my lack of volume control.

The first time I noticed that my speech was slurred was when I returned home from a speech therapy session in White Plains, New York and listened to a message I had left on my answering machine. The second time I was made aware of my changing speech patterns was when I was talking to a girlfriend who has ataxia as well, and she pointed out that difference.

Tremors are caused by muscle contractions and relaxation. My head could tremor at any time, day or night. It would shake side to side. Head tremors are annoying. My head shakes more when I am fatigued. I attempt to control the shaking by resting my head on the back of the sofa when sitting in the family room.

Sometimes I experience tremors in my right hand when I am reading. Needless to say, it is quite difficult to read while the book or newspaper or magazine is moving!

Anxiety, stress, and fatigue make both types of tremors more obvious. I have found that resting relaxes me and reduces the severity of the tremors. Also, taking deep breaths is calming to my body.

"And be not conformed to this world…but transformed by the renewing of your mind, ye may prove what is that good and acceptable and perfect will of God."
Romans 12:2

Chapter 4

Accepting Life as It Comes

You may ask, what does "accepting life" mean? "Life" refers to the occurrences or anything that may happen during one's earthly existence. The occurrence may be planned or unplanned, but often situations that are unforeseen can create sadness and fear, and even hardship.

Regardless of how devastating a life event or experience is, one should confront it with a positive attitude, looking forward to improvement in one's circumstances, and banking on an ultimately favorable outcome.

The best way to accomplish this is to talk to someone whom you feel comfortable confiding in, someone whom you consider trustworthy. Be proactive; read related materials about those who have encountered similar difficulty. Start a support group, and/or document your personal experiences to help others.

It doesn't matter what sort of situation you are dealing with. What is most important is how well you can make positive adjustments and create ways to manage and cope, and in so doing, triumph over your challenges.

I do not consider myself a cockeyed optimist; far from it. I understand that for all of us, acceptance of the hardships of life in any form is difficult.

<u>Serenity Prayer</u>

**God grant me
the serenity to accept
the things I cannot change,
the courage to change the things I can,
and the wisdom to know the difference.**

Author Unknown

A strong spiritual belief, the love and support of family and friends, along with a positive attitude will help us cope with life-altering conditions.

"Lord, give me the gift of faith to be renewed and shared with others each day. Teach me to live this moment only, looking neither to the past with regret, nor the future with apprehension. Let love be my aim and my life prayer." *Roseann Alexander-Isham*

Talking to others about their real-life experiences is so rewarding. I had the pleasure of meeting a man in his late forties who appeared to be completely and positively accepting of an acute life change, and he is coping quite well. In a matter of minutes, his life had been turned upside down when, because of an environmental issue, he ended up in the hospital with fluid accumulating in his brain, unable to walk, hear, or see out of one eye.

In spite of such a traumatic circumstance, he spoke excitedly about the delights of having a growing young family, comprised of a beautiful wife and two young boys.

"Happy is the man that findeth wisdom, and the man that getteth understanding."

Proverbs 3:13

Chapter 5

Dare to Be Happy!

Happiness is a state of mind, to be protected. Each of us is responsible for our own happiness. Take ownership of your happiness. A life filled with happiness is also filled with joy.

One's mind, body and soul is in harmony.

Each day, affirm out loud the things that make you happy. Visualize those things, and the things that you are blessed with. Make a list of them.

My list includes the following, but it is by no means limited to these:

- A strong belief in a higher power (Jesus Christ)

- A positive attitude or outlook on life

- Creating and maintaining positive relationships with family and friends

- Reaching out to others in a positive manner; the more you give, the more that is given back to you.

Listen to what most relaxes and calms you, for example, sounds of birds singing, children playing, or ocean waves, either with the real thing or utilizing CDs.

Think and act positive. Flood your mind with positive thoughts. Expect positive results from everything you do. Do not allow negative thoughts that will prevent you from being happy to enter your mind. Affirm out loud each day that you are going to be happy.

Don't worry about or entertain fears about things that

are beyond your control. Put your mind at rest. Take control of your life.

Start by putting a smile on your face. Then say, "Hello!"

If you are in a beauty salon, for example, compliment someone on their hair. If you are in a shopping mall, comment to the elderly lady resting on a bench what a lovely scarf she is wearing.

If you are in a nail salon, compliment a stranger on their choice of nail color. One afternoon I was waiting to get my nails done, and instead of burying my face in a magazine, I said hello to a man who came in to the shop to pick up his wife.

"Hello! How are you?" He was astonished and delighted at the same time.

"No one ever says hello to me." He became animated, and we had a short but very pleasant conversation.

Do not be controlled by a desire to turn away and ignore others. Make the effort to be positive. You have no idea how much impact you can make with three simple words, "How are you?"

These are simple acts of kindness. They make the recipient happy, and you come away with a serene sense of satisfaction.

"…he whoever trust in the Lord, happy is he."
Proverbs 16:20

"Show us Your mercy,
Lord, and grant us Your salvation."
Psalm 85:7

Chapter 6

Never Take Anything for Granted

I once attended a banquet where the food was served buffet-style on seemingly never-ending tables.

I sat in renewed appreciation and amazement, as my fellow attendees deftly balanced plates of food and beverages while at the same time walking back to their tables without spilling a morsel or a drop. In the meanwhile, my husband left me seated at our table and in a few minutes miraculously returned with a plate filled with goodies, a simple act that ataxia prevents me from doing.

It was clear that the majority of the guests took their ability to walk and carry a plate of food for granted.

Several years ago, I lost the ability to do the many simple, everyday things that would have allowed me to function as a "normal" person. Now, I never take the ability to do anything for granted. I pray to God that, one day, my health will be restored.

Ataxia has slowly robbed me of physical functions such as those listed below:

- o Balancing
- o Walking
- o Carrying a cup or glass filled with liquid
- o Writing
- o Talking
- o Standing
- o Dressing

I have always wondered, is it better to have a disability and slowly lose the ability to perform certain tasks, or is it better to have never been able to do those things, such as balancing or walking?

You can't miss what you never had. Quite a thought-provoking statement.

God is the source of all things. Count your blessings. Things could be a lot worse. Many of us are familiar with the person who complained they didn't have any shoes until they saw a man who didn't have any feet.

My suggestion is to approach any illness or disability, regardless of severity, in a positive way, and handle the difficulties resulting from the problem condition with optimism and in a proactive manner. The first step toward healing is acceptance.

A proactive attitude and response to a serious condition or situation involves the following:

- Documenting one's experiences

- Reading as much as possible about the characteristics of the situation

- Joining a support group to share common issues with others in the same boat

•

"For I will restore health to you and heal you of your wounds, says the Lord."
Jeremiah 30:17

"Blessed be the God and Father of our Lord Jesus Christ, who hath blessed us with all spiritual blessing in heavenly places in Christ."
Ephesians 1:3

"Blessed be the Lord, because he hath heard the voice of my supplications. The Lord is my strength and my shield; my heart trusted in him, and I am helped; therefore, my heart greatly rejoiceth; and with my song will praise him."
Psalm 28:6-8

"Blessed be God, even the Father of our Lord Jesus Christ, the Father of mercies, and the God of all comfort, who comforteth us in all our tribulations, that we may be able to comfort them which are in any trouble, by the comfort wherewith we ourselves are comforted of God."
II Corinthians 1:3-4

"For we walk by faith, not by sight."
II Corinthians 5:7

Chapter 7
Keeping the Faith

Faith is a term, used in a spiritual way, to express one's commitment and belief in the guidance of the Kingdom of God. Webster's Dictionary defines faith as the unquestioning belief in God that does not require proof or evidence.

Faith is of the heart, and it is acquired through the Holy Spirit, i.e., the divine influence or inspiration of God. One grows in faith through reading and meditating on God's word. One's faith also grows by hearing and believing God's word. We can increase our faith in God by studying His word and experiencing the testimony of others.

My faith in the Lord has been steadfast, and I glorify His name on a continuous basis.

The Bible teaches us that Jesus was commanded by His Father God to shed His blood on the cross for the world's (my) sins, and He honored His Father's wishes completely. We can not please God if we don't believe in Him. Through the readings of His word, we know he is the creator of all things. His love for each of us is unconditional and bountiful, and He is all-powerful.

The fundamental belief of Christians is that Jesus, the son of God, died on the cross. Jesus shed his blood for the sins of man so that all mankind would be saved.

Divine faith in almighty God comes from listening to, reading, and studying His Gospel, which leads to renewing one's mind in the Holy Spirit.

"Now faith is the substance of things hoped for, the evidence of things not seen."
Hebrews 11:1

"So then faith cometh by hearing, and hearing by the word of God."
Romans 10:17

"But without faith it is impossible to please him; for he that cometh to God must believe that he is and that he is a rewarder of them that diligently seek him."
Hebrews 11:6

"Through faith we understand that the worlds were framed by the word of God, so that things which are seen were not made of things which do appear."
Hebrews 11:3

"This is My (God's) commandment, that ye love one another, as I have loved you. Greater love hath no man than this, that a man lay down his life for his friends."
John 15:12-13

"But that the world may know that I love the Father, and as the Father gave me commandment, even so I do."
John 14:31

"Do not conform to this world but be ye transformed by the renewing of your mind, that ye may prove what is that good and acceptable and perfect, will of God."
Romans 12:2

"For God so loved the world, that he gave his only begotten Son, that whosoever believeth in Him should not perish, but have everlasdting life."
John 3:16

"Show us Your mercy, Lord, and grant us Your salvation."
Psalm 85:7

*"God, give me peace of mind to
live with the things I cannot alter,
The strength to make different the things I can,
And wisdom to understand which things I can change
and which ones I cannot."*

Chapter 8
Peace of Mind

Some people confuse achieving peace of mind, being in a state of tranquility and calm, with the ability to escape reality or run from their troubles.

Norman Pearle's *Stay Alive All Your Life* deals with this very subject. I concur with his view, that peace of mind is a temporary state of being where one can rid the mind of negative thoughts and restore it with:

- Energy
- Power
- Clear thoughts
- Calmness

The process includes imagining being at one's favorite place, emptying the mind, and freeing oneself of constricting or uncomfortable clothing. I perform this procedure of clearing my mind each time I consider writing a new book. Early preparation for me involves a calm self-examination and review of my abilities to start, develop, and ultimately complete a project. This allows me to tackle a major undertaking like book writing, and succeed without getting lost in the negative and vicious cycle of "what-if."

I assess various aspects of my physical and mental readiness:

- **Health** -- Do I have a history of becoming ill while under stress? Can I finish producing the book within a reasonable time frame?

- **Tremor** --Do my hands and head shake uncontrollably?

- **Mental capabilities** -- I know they are good, but can they handle the intensity of the project without setting myself up for exhaustion?

Once this self-analysis step is completed, I move on:

- Step 2: I make an outline along with a rough draft of the table of contents.

- Step 3: I focus on the table of contents again and again, to be sure the various items are pertinent and significant. The topics will often change.

- Step 4: I begin writing the body of the text, generally working on one topic, not necessarily in the order it appears in the book, skipping to another topic, and eventually returning to previous chapters for revision.

At least once a month, we need to practice getting into a peaceful state of mind to address difficult and possibly high-stress decisions like what to do about one or more aspects of our current and future physical, mental, or emotional situations.

I am particularly peaceful when I acknowledge the presence of God in my life. Studying the Bible and meditating on God's word, my entire being is spiritually uplifted.

"The Lord is my helper;
I will not fear.
What can man do to me?"
Hebrews 13:6

Chapter 9
Facing Your Fears

The concept of "peace of mind" applies here. One can empty one's mind of fearsome thoughts or any kind of negative influence.

The Lord's Prayer is very familiar to many people. I often read it to stop negative thoughts from invading my mind and taking over, so to speak. I also turn to the 23rd Psalm if someone has done harm to me or a member of my family.

A process I found extremely helpful in keeping me grounded, purposeful and positive is committing favorite Bible verses to memory. That way, I always have my inspiration with me:

"I will fear no evil, for Thou art with me."

Another powerful Bible verse that is among my favorites is the prayer that Jesus taught his disciples. I like to both read and meditate on this passage when I become fearful or uncertain:

"Our Father in heaven, hallowed be Thy name.

Thy Kingdom come…"

Matthew 6:9-13

Do not allow useless thoughts to enter your mind. Thoughts born of fear are usually based on unsubstantiated information that is useless and a waste of energy. They are thoughts about circumstances that we have no control over. Put your time and energy to good and positive use by thinking of ways to make your daily life easier, in light of your situation.

Fear thoughts. Like many people with ataxia, I am afraid of losing my independence and having to continually look to others for my needs. There are many forms this fear can take. Young mothers with ataxia wonder whether their ability to care for their babies and children will be compromised to the point where others need to step in.

"The fear of man brings a snare. But whoever trust in the Lord shall be safe."
Proverbs 29:25

"Fear not, for I am with you…"
Isaiah 43:5

"But I say unto you, love your enemies, bless them that curse you, do good to them that hate you, and pray for them which despitefully use you, and persecute you."
Matthew 5:44

"I will restore health to you and heal you of your wounds, says the Lord."
Jeremiah 30:17

Chapter 10
A Healing Prayer

Healing is the process or act of making something better by removing the substance or element which causes a disruption in the correct and positive functioning of a physical or emotional state.

Christians refer to the belief in and personal use of the positive powers of God as faith healing. Many people define faith as the unquestioning belief in God, requiring neither proof nor "hard" evidence. Faith in God increases through reading the Bible and hearing testimony about His healing energy.

One's faith in God's healing power should be strong, steadfast, and sure.

Before receiving the gift of divine healing, one must first believe they are in fact going to be healed through the Holy Spirit of God. A willingness to accept God's word is all that is required for healing to begin. God heals the sick and makes the weak strong.

God's love for me was revealed thousands of years before I was born, when Jesus died in Calvary on the cross so that I and all of mankind would be saved. God is a loving God, a forgiving God, a merciful God. His divine powers created the heaven and the earth.

Almighty God, hear my prayer. God, I come to you just as I am, broken in health, but not in my faith.

Father God, I have survived this far through faith, leaning on You all the way and trusting in Your Holy Spirit for divine guidance. And I will continue to do so forever.

You know my every need. Oh, God, restore me to health. I have faith in Your healing powers. I believe that I will receive healing.

According to Your divine plan, I patiently wait to be made new again.

Strengthen my compassion for others in need; my ability to recognize those who bear heavy burdens; my desire to comfort them, just as you have comforted me so many times, in so many ways. Strengthen also my desire to continue to grow in faith and to walk in the path of righteousness. Strengthen my desire to love others just as You love me.

In Your name, I pray. Amen.

"Now, faith is the substance of things hoped for, the evidence of things not seen."
Hebrews 11:1

"I will restore health to you and heal you of your wounds, says the Lord."
Jeremiah 30:17

"Therefore I say unto you, what things soever ye desire, when ye pray, believe that ye receive them, and ye shall have them."
Mark 11:24

"...for your Father knows the things you have need of before you ask Him."

Matthew 6:8

"Blessed be the Lord, because He hath heard the voice of my supplications. The Lord is my strength and my shield; my heart trusted in Him, and I am helped; therefore my heart greatly rejoiceth; and with my song will praise Him."

Psalm 28:6-8

"Finally, my brethren, be strong in the Lord, and in the power of His might."
Ephesians 6:10

Chapter 11
Moving on with My Life

The decision to move on with your life reflects a resolve to accept your present situation while at the same time anticipating a positive outcome.

Evaluate your circumstances as they are now, and make new plans in accordance with newly drawn goals and objectives. Determine the best and most direct way to achieve them. Consider going back to school with the intent to acquire additional marketable skills through training either in the same field or another field of interest.

If mobility issues are a consideration, rearrange your home to make it more accessible and easier to manage. Start with small changes and work steadily toward a major overhaul. Make similar alterations to your work space, both in the home and in the office.

If you are a wheelchair user, ensure that kitchen utensils, clothes, toiletries or anything you deem to be of importance in everyday living are at a lower height and within easy reach. Install handicap bars on both sides of the toilet, at the head and on the sides of the tub, on three sides of the shower stall. Have a long hose installed to allow for comfortable showering while seated in a waterproof chair.

Making changes like these does not mean one is giving up or giving in to the medical condition; on the contrary, these are acts of pure self-empowerment and self-determination.

I will meet all future challenges, physical or emotional,

with a positive attitude. I believe that the way we view good and bad life experiences influences our ability to deal with them. A continually positive attitude will yield continually positive results.

Make arrangements with a spouse and/or friend to do grocery and other shopping, to assist in attending doctor appointments, to pay bills, to arrange for housecleaning, and to make it possible to go to church.

Until we take the time to appreciate today and all its many blessings, we won't be adequately prepared to appreciate tomorrow.

"So don't be anxious about tomorrow. God will take care of your tomorrow, too. Live one day at a time."
Matthew 6:34

"Trust in the Lord with all thine heart; and lean not unto thine own understanding. In all thy ways acknowledge Him, and He shall direct thy paths."
Proverbs 3:5-6

"But without faith it is impossible to please Him; for he that cometh to God must believe that He is and He is a rewarder of them that diligently seek Him."
Hebrews 11:6

"For I will restore health to you and heal you of your wounds, says the Lord."

Jeremiah 30:17

"Train up a child in the way he should go, and when he is old he will not depart from it."
Proverbs 22:6

Chapter 12
Children Living with Disabilities

Several years ago, while searching in the children's book sections of libraries and bookstores, I quickly and sadly realized how few children's books dealing with disabilities are available.

Books of this nature can be invaluable to children who are themselves disabled, and also in helping youngsters not debilitated by a physical or mental problem learn to understand, appreciate and respect the challenges faced by their disabled peers.

Children like to read books about a lifestyle similar to their own. Realizing that the child in the story has a disability like theirs reassures the reader that they are not alone, and they share a common bond with that book's characters.

An atmosphere must be created in the books that will foster positive interaction between disabled and able-bodied people. This design will promote diversity by inviting and embracing it, and focusing on the need for acceptance of people's differences.

It is my opinion that misguided and/or erroneous attitudes toward physically and emotionally challenged people have to change, and that change must begin at the most basic level: with our children. It is through the positive efforts of all people that we will change the negative social perception of people who are, in one way or another, different.

I propose that we start with positive parental role models reflecting a positive attitude of acceptance that children will surely emulate. Books mirroring that attitude will not only bolster the confidence and self-esteem of children living with the challenges of disability, it will make the world a much better place.

Chapter 13
Exercising

Regular exercise is beneficial to us all. We should exercise at least fifteen to twenty minutes daily and at least four times a week. It is especially important for a person with spinal cerebellar ataxia, who is likely to have muscle weakness and loss of coordination in his or her legs and arms, as well as loss of flexibility in the joints.

Exercise reduces the risk of serious medical issues such as heart disease, diabetes, and high blood pressure, to name a few.

Fatigue is one of several symptoms of ataxia. Alternating exercise with appropriate rest energizes the body, and creates pathways for healing. How much exercise I do and the type of exercise I perform depends on my energy level at the time. I exercise at a pace that is comfortable for me. When I get tired, I stop! I have learned to listen to my body. I do not continue physical exertion of any kind when my body protests.

Stretching helps me maintain good muscle tone and flexibility. I never over-stretch my muscles because it can be painful and can result in serious injury. Muscles should be stretched a little at a time.

Walking enhances both my flexibility and relaxation. I like to walk because I can do it at my own pace, and I can do it alone or with a friend. When the weather is nice, I walk in the morning when it is still cool and after the neighborhood children have gone to school. When I walk outside, I walk at a slower pace, about two and a half miles per hour for sixty minutes.

When the weather is bad, I walk indoors on a treadmill. I enjoy walking on the treadmill because I can measure distance, speed, time, and other factors about my walk. I have maintained a log book for more than fifteen years to record when I exercise, for how long, the types of exercises performed, my weight, the number of glasses of water I drink each day, and other physical health factors I feel are important to track.

Pool exercising is an excellent way to achieve a workout goal. When the water is a comfortable temperature, I do some of my stretching in the pool. Walking in chest-deep water is a good way to work toward aerobic fitness. The water resistance and buoyancy make it easier to exercise.

I always practice good safety habits in and round the pool. If it is available, I hold on to a railing or the like that affords support for me as I get in and out of the pool. I never get into the pool without someone around in case I need assistance.

I cannot stress too much the importance of exercise.

Exercise should be done at your own speed and within your own capabilities. I don't spend time and energy dwelling on the exercises I can no longer do. I simply work at those that I can do without excessive strain, which can lead to injury.

Consult with your doctor before starting an exercise program. A medical professional will advise you of the most beneficial type of exercises for you, when you should do them, and how frequently. Follow that advice, and guide your body to the best it can be.

Facial Stretch

Objective: To stretch the muscles in your face and to stimulate the muscles in the tongue

- Open your mouth as wide as possible
- Move your jaw up and down, and rotate your jaw around, as if you were drawing an invisible circle with your chin
- Stick your tongue out as far as it will go
- Rotate your tongue in a circle while outstreatched, tracing the shape of your opened mouth
- Open your eyes as widely as you can, stretching the muscles in the back of the eyes
- Relax
- Repeat this exercise as often as you feel comfortable

Head Twist

Objective: To relieve tension in your neck

- This exercise can be done almost anywhere from a seated position (except when driving)
- Twist your head slowly to the right, looking over the right shoulder
- Hold that stretch for fifteen to twenty seconds
- Relax
- Repeat this exercise by twisting slowly to the left
- Repeat the entire exercise as often as you feel comfortable

Over-the-Head Arm Stretch
Objective: To achieve a total body stretch
- Sit erect or stand tall
- Pull stomach in for back support
- Slowly raise both arms high above your head and stretch as if you are attempting to touch the ceiling
- Hold the stretch for fifteen to twenty seconds
- Slowly lower both arms to your sides
- Relax
- Repeat this exercise three times

Bilateral (Both) Arm Rotations
Objective: To gain arm strength
- Sit erect, or stand (I prefer the seated position)
- Pull stomach in for back support
- Stretch both arms out to the side, shoulder height, and pretend to reach for the walls on either side of you
- Make small circles with your outstretched arms. Do not bend the elbows.
- Gradually increase the size of the circle with each rotation
- Relax
- Repeat this exercise three times

Hand and Wrist Flex
Objective: To exercise both hands and wrists
- Hold both arms out to the sides, elbows locked. Raise arms until hands are parallel with your waist
- Stretch fingers apart
- Close and open hands
- Flex wrist by keeping fingers together and, without moving the arms, point fingers up as far as you are comfortable, then downward
- Relax
- Repeat this exercise as often as you feel comfortable

Waist Twist
Objective: To exercise hips and back
- Lay down on the floor on your back
- Pull stomach in to support back
- Stretch both arms out on either side of the body
- Pull both knees up to stomach
- Roll slowly from side to side
- Repeat exercise for ten to fifteen minutes
- Relax

Calves, Ankles and Toes Flex
Objective: To stretch the calves, ankles and toes
- Sit down on a chair, feet facing forward
- Take shoes off
- Sit erect; pull stomach in to support back

- Slide both feet back toward yourself
- Then slide feet away from yourself as far forward as possible, pointing toes
- Hold for ten or fifteen seconds; release and allow feet to come back to a normal resting position
- Wiggle the toes
- Spread toes apart
- Squeeze toes; release and allow feet to come back to a normal resting position
- Flex ankles, first pointing toes up while keeping the legs still, then pointing toes down
- Relax
- Repeat exercises three times

Thigh Stretch
Objective: To stretch the thigh muscles
- Lie down face up on floor
- Hold stomach in for lower back support
- Roll over on to left side
- Bend right leg back and grab right ankle with right hand
- Pull foot toward buttock slowly
- Hold for fifteen to twenty seconds; release
- Roll over on to right side
- Repeat exercise for the left leg
- Relax
- Repeat exercise three times

Calves and Back Stretch/Abdominal Crunch
Objective: To stretch the lower back, the calf muscle, and to help flatten the stomach

- Sit erect on floor, legs straight out in front
- Pull stomach in to support lower back
- Pull heels together until they touch
- Reach to grasp feet with hands, making sure elbows are between legs as you lean forward
- Press thighs toward floor
- Hold for fifteen to twenty seconds
- Relax
- Repeat this exercise three times

Shoulder Lifts
Objective: To help flatten the stomach

- Lie down on the floor on your back
- Find a point on the ceiling to focus on
- Pull stomach in to support lower back
- For further back support, bend knees with feet flat on floor
- Place hands behind head and lift shoulders a few inches off the floor, staying focused on the point on the ceiling
- Do not bend your head and neck. Keep head, neck and shoulders moving as one unit to achieve maximum benefit
- Do three sets of twenty-five to start, progressing at your own pace
- Relax

Knee Crunch
Objective: To help flatten stomach

- Lie on back on the floor
- Pull stomach in to support lower back
- Raise knees to stomach
- Grab knees with both hands and press knees to stomach
- Hold stretch for fifteen to twenty seconds
- Relax
- Repeat this exercise three times

Leg Lifts
Objective: To strengthen leg muscles

- Lie on back on the floor
- Roll on to right side
- Keeping left leg straight but not stiff, slowly lift it as high as possible
- Slowly lower the left leg, stopping a few inches from the floor
- Hold for ten or fifteen seconds
- Lower the left leg to the floor and relax
- Roll on to left side and repeat with the right leg
- Repeat this exercise three times

Cobra
Objective: To stretch the entire spine

- Place small cloth or face towel on the floor

- Lie on stomach on the floor

- Hold stomach in to support lower back

- Place forehead on floor and place hands, palms down, fingers of each hand together and pointing toward the other, between the shoulders and the floor

- Relax

- Slowly push down on hands and lift your upper body as far as it can comfortably go (spine is curved)

- Hold in this position for ten to twenty seconds

- Slowly come back down to rest on the floor

- Relax

- Repeat this exercise three times

Flat-out Relax
Objective: To bring the entire body and mind to a state of calm

- Lie on your back

- Rest your arms at your sides

- Close your eyes

- *Empty your mind of all thoughts*

- Relax

- This exercise can also be done while sitting

- Repeat as often as you like

Trying to Balance

Focus on BALANCING.
Getting up every morning,
I stumble to the bathroom. It is hard to balance.
Three or four steps, I am okay,
Leaning on the wall to shower and dress.
It is hard because I cannot balance!
Oh! I drop the soap…
Careful; don't fall!
I cannot balance.
Walking…trying to keep my balance;
Going up and down steps, trying to balance.
Riding a bicycle?
No, I cannot balance!
Carrying a cup of tea?
It is hard because I cannot balance!
I miss being able to balance.

February 5, 1994

Exercising at the Crack of Dawn

Exercising every morning

At the crack of dawn,

Walking to the rhythm of the music I start.

Thirty minutes I go,

Sometimes for sixty minutes,

Depending on the way I am feeling.

I exercise to stay flexible.

ARE YOU EXERCISING?

February 5, 1994

Ataxians Speak

Below are some comments from various individuals afflicted with ataxia. They are unedited remarks about this disease and its role in the lives of these people. Their names are shown only as initials to protect their privacy.

Question: **"As ataxians, what do you fear most?"**

FA: Most ataxians are scared of change, becoming dependent on others, i.e., losing one's independence such as being unable to drive a car, prepare meals, and even worse, for me, having to give up my privacy when using the toilet.

GH: Right now, things are good for me. I can still walk, drive and pretty much do for myself. But things might change at any moment, and it scares the heck out of me. I know I have a lot of support from my family, but I'm afraid of losing my independence and having to ask for help with the things I can do now. I try to stay positive and hope things will be okay for me.

PB: It's hard not to look forward in fear, just as it's hard not to look backward with regret. Yes, the future can be very scary, even more so in our circumstances. But if this disease has given me anything, it's the appreciation of the present.

The fact is, no matter how bad my bad days seem now, one day I'll look back on these times as the good old days when it wasn't that bad! That can be it's own heartache as well, as I think of opportunities missed and time wasted because I didn't know what was coming and what was happening to me, and I didn't take advantage of the ability I had at the time.

LS: I feel it is a blessing. I have learned so much, not just about this disease, but about the importance of compassion towards others. I have always thought of myself as a compassionate person, but ataxia has opened my eyes to a greater appreciation of life. I know things might get rough, but I feel we all have a purpose in life, and I have found mine.

CC: Ataxia is a symptom, not a specific disease or diagnosis. "Ataxia" means clumsiness or loss of coordination. Ataxia can affect the fingers and hands, the arms or legs, the body, speech or movement of the eyes. This loss of coordination may be caused by a number of different medical or neurological conditions.

Yes, ataxia can cause you to fall, but with what you say, I'd suspect the medication might be the source of that falling, and I'd check with my doctor right away.

*   *   *

It is interesting to read about the feelings and opinions of other people living with ataxia. I belong to an online group of ataxians who live all over the world. This chat space provides a wealth of information about different forms of ataxia, their symptoms and their side effects. Mobility aids are discussed and evaluated.

*   *   *

Question: **Do you ever fall?**

RT: I fell around March 18th, fell straight down hard, to the right of the dog cage near the entrance to the kitchen, right into the family room. I ended up with a long staple in my right hand. It's April 10th, and it still hurts, so I made an appointment with the orthopedist on April 24th. My right knee is bruised and it also still hurts. My knees are getting so weak, sometimes it feels like my right knee is twisted.

Question: **Do you have heart-related problems?**

KS: I am so confused and don't know what to do. I had an echo a month ago and it showed my cardiac function has declined to an ejection fraction of 29%. My doc wanted to be exact, so I had a Muga on Tuesday of this week. The Muga showed my EF to be really 27%. He has sent in a referral to get a defibrillator and has told me to double my ace inhibitor and my beta blocker.

I am confused as to whether I should start Idebenone or not. Of course, the doc says it's not FDA approved and we don't know if it will work or not and what the side effects are, etc. He made a comment about, we don't know what it will do in 20 years.

After I left, I thought, well, I don't care about 20 years from now, because if the meds he's giving me now don't want to work anymore, I won't be here in 20 years anyway! I did tell him I wanted to be tested in six months and not once a year anymore.

I said if the doubling of the medications I'm on now don't work in the next six months, then I'm going on Idebenone. I figure I'll have nothing to lose and I may gain some more time. I just would really like to know your opinions on starting it now, or should I wait for six months? Thanks.

Question: **How would you describe what your days are like, good and/or bad?**

DI: A couple of years ago, I met a young lady who uses a Lightwriter. Her speech was so slurred that I could not understand her. Of course, my hearing is not that great a times, so that also could have been a factor. My friend was with me, and he could understand her a bit better than I. Anyway, the reason I am writing is I thought the device was terrific, even if it is just used to break the ice with new people until they can get accustomed to your voice. Looking for a device like this is partly because I have become much more self-conscious about my speech, nervous that others are listening to me and afraid I won't be understood.

*   *   *

TF: I am neither a proponent nor averse to homeopathy, but as a pharmacist, I would like to talk about my personal experience with homeopathy.

In the beginning of my SCA, I was very much worried and depressed. Sedatives and antidepressants helped, but they also would blur my brain and dull my thinking abilities. At that time, I consulted a good homeopath who prescribed a drug for me according to my personality.

The drug worked wonders, and after three to four months I had not a trace of anxiety or depression, and no allopathic drugs. Now I have been prescribed Conium which has decreased my tremors 30 to 40% in four months.

It remains to be seen what will happen in the future. I am also taking my allopathic drugs as such, with no alteration in dosage.

AG: I was going to give a long speech about all the reasons why homeopathy can't and doesn't work, but then I thought, why waste energy. You say you're a pharmacist, so I'll take your word for it. Then you know that homeopathy is nothing but hogwash.

As a person with a hereditary form of ataxia myself and as a member of Internaf, I make it my duty to denounce quackery when I see it.

*   *   *

BD: The typical procedure used to correct some of the foot deformity associated with ataxia is called a triple arthrodesis and does not involve the fusion of the ankle joint, but three joints that are located in the hind foot above the heel. It gives stability to the foot so the ankle is less prone to "turn over."

I had the surgery when I was 19, along with a lengthening of the first metatarsal bones of each foot to reduce a high arch. I was ambulatory until age 42, and the surgery afforded a lot of benefit to me, even now that I am a wheelchair user. I had several nasty sprains before the surgery and a lot of pain whenever I did a lot of standing or walking. I worked up until age 37.

If your doctor is recommending a complete ankle fusion, that is a different procedure altogether, usually done on a severely arthritic ankle. Good luck!

*   *   *

MM: I have cerebellar ataxia and I am going back to see my doctor in November for a checkup. I am not sure which type I have, as my doctor is still testing me. I have slowly, progressively gotten worse. My walking and balancing is like a drunken sailor. I am stumbling and have vision, hearing and other problems.

I do have arthritis which is causing some of my problems, but tests show I have ataxia also. I no longer drive or work, so I am home all the time. It has been a big lifestyle change. I have some good days and some down days.

There is no support group, so it is nice to get on the email and chat with others like myself. Take care. I am glad to be here to share and learn with all of you.

Question: **What is the condition of restless legs?**

AN: I noticed a conversation on here about restless legs. Sometimes I have that too. They jump occasionally by themselves as well. Sometimes I'll have muscle spasms in them so painful I can barely stop from screaming.

For the last month, I have been having pain in my legs at night when I go to bed. It really feels more like a pressure on them. My legs throb a lot, especially around the ankles and at the back of the knees. I had been taking COQ-10 regularly for the past two months or so, and I thought maybe that would improve the circulation in my legs. The pain was so intense that it kept me from sleeping.

I decided to stop the COQ-10 for a few days now. My legs have stopped throbbing at night, but for the past two days, when I go to stand, I can't support myself anymore. When I stand and attempt to transfer weight to my legs, they feel like they aren't even there. It takes a few moments and even a few tries to be able to stay standing. I have only been able to stand and transfer my weight once or twice by myself in the past few days.

It's very scary. And tonight, just now, when I stood in the bathroom and attempted to transfer my weight, a searing pain shot right behind my knee, especially when I tried to put my full weight on my left leg.

I was wondering if anyone had ever experienced anything like this. I have no idea if it's anything to do with the COQ-10 or not. Perhaps it has nothing to do with it at all. Could it just be a progression of the disease? Is this a stage of FA (Friedrich's taxia)? I guess only FA-ers can answer that, but maybe you guys with other forms of ataxia might have experienced this issue.

*   *   *

RB: I've read with interest all the replies I got. I'm pleasantly surprised to read your stories. There are older ataxians doing well; middle-aged ones married, with children; some actively in the work force; in short, leading virtually normal lives! And I've discovered this since I joined this group and started hearing from ataxians in other countries.

I don't know, Spain must be different. Before joining Internaf, I just knew about Spanish ataxians, people 30, 40, 50, who lived with their parents and brothers/sisters who were also affected, sexually inactive, spending their lives indoors all day, online, doing little else. Only the younger ataxians had an active life. I don't know if it's due to fear or the lack of self-confidence, but the older ones seem surrendered to their isolation.

I felt really rare among them, because I have had and still have much to do. I wanted to tell them to make the most of their lives now, without dwelling on what the future will bring. I know that ataxia is a progressive disease; I know there's no cure; but while I can, it will not stop me from being truly ALIVE!

Society in general doesn't help you much, nor does the government. People underestimate you; sometimes members of your own family don't believe in you, or trust you to be a fully contributing individual. As a result, you can do two things: accept their opinion of your shortcomings, or rebel and be yourself. Some ataxians lose self-confidence and end up being physically and emotionally dependent because they are convinced they can't do very much. Others, like me, fight everybody, even myself at times, because it is so unfair that I have to have a severely controlled life where often those not affected by this disease treat me with little or no respect.

For example, say you are a young and attractive person, but disabled, in a wheelchair. You meet someone who is not disabled and you both fall in love. People may comment that you just want someone to help you and take you places, or they say that the "normal" half of the couple just wants to deceive you, get your money, or have some romantic fun at your expense.

I have suffered that many times, especially with my present boyfriend who I adore. It hurts a lot. But I couldn't run away. I had to hear them, and I cried when I was alone in my room. How can I forgive all that? How can I stand it?

*   *   *

PH: Thank you for starting such a terrific discussion.

I was interested in the following topic, not only as a person with SCA6, but I happen to be writing a thinly-veiled fictitious novel about a woman facing this exact question: **What would you do if your doctor offered a cure?**

In this story, family and friends are astounded and perplexed that she has any second thoughts at all.

Some of you hit on one of the central issues: What about work? I have spent YEARS adapting to being housebound and accepted giving up a promising career as a research neuroscientist and college professor. I now teach part-time online, and I have adjusted well.

I like being able to teach in my pajamas and on my own schedule. I think it has been a year since I even put on pantyhose! I just donated much of my work clothes and shoes to charity, even though I have been working at home for three years. Acceptance was slow for me and is for many others. But I never intended to end up this way.

I have adjusted well. If not for ataxia, I would probably still be smoking a pack of cigarettes a day, working 60 to 80 hours per week (trying to, as they say, "publish, or perish" in academia). I probably would not be doing yoga daily, eating a good diet, being a fanatic about fitness. I actually owe these good things to ataxia.

Would I really want to return to the rat race? Maybe, but only on my terms, and not losing any of the things that ataxia has taught me.

And let's be *real* honest. There is a certain attractiveness to the sick role. I try never to exploit my condition, but I'd be less than honest if I said that the appearance of a debilitating condition does not have its benefits. Would I be willing to give them up? You bet. But, in truth, I would miss them sometimes.

The dreams are great: running, dancing…but really, one spends years adjusting to life with a serious illness. To think that if things were suddenly reversed and I was returned to complete health, I think I'd do more than just dance.

JD: It is the adjustment to ill health that interests me. Not just the dreams; I have those too. I live right across the street from the beach, yet I have not walked on the sand in years. Yes, I'm lucky (and grateful) to be here, but it does break my heart not to be able to walk along the shore. Every time I look out at the ocean, I appreciate its beauty. But I never forget that my enjoyment of it now is limited in ways that only a cure could change.

So if I were cured, I would take a long walk on the beach, and then jump into the surf!

I know there would be much more than that to do. I'd have to consider what to do about work. I'd have to give up the sympathy factor, including those who think I'm a brave and courageous soul because of my battle with ataxia. I'd have to be brave and courageous based on my own merits again. And I'm sure I'd have to work very hard to retain everything I have learned as a result of having ataxia.

I think all of us with serious illness are unwilling members of a special club. We know things that healthy people do not. We hate having to have learned these things, but we had to. I think un-joining this club might be harder than we realize. Do you have any thoughts?

PH: I realize full well that many of you, especially those with FA, never had a chance to do much of what I did, having a relatively late-onset (mid-30s) version of the disease. I am sensitive to that. But this issue also begs the question: Is it easier to give up what you had, or is it easier never having had those things at all? It is a ridiculous question, to be sure. But still, like the *what-if,* we ask it, no matter how unanswerable. We still ask.

Maybe the cure question is equally fruitless. It is just a hypothetical. But I think it is a very important question to keep asking. One day it *will* be answered. It's important not to just consider the dreams we could realize, but the challenges of being healthy.

Keep having those dreams. I know I do. Right now my most vivid vision is that a cure is found in time for my son, who is at 50 percent risk. I can only dream about what is possible FOR ME today.

"Ask wisely, with love, for everything you want."

I agree. I am the only child of seven children who has ataxia. I try to keep a positive attitude. I feel that knowledge is power, so I read books on coping in general.

Reading through your attachment was like going down memory lane for me…what I used to be like. I could have substituted my name with different dates into your personal history. Your experience is virtually identical to my early years.

You can look to your mom to some degree as to what to expect, but I inherited this from my father, and I have done things completely differently in every respect, so that I am much better off then he was at the same stage of this disease. Let's just say that he had a bad attitude about life before being diagnosed with ataxia. The disease did nothing to improve him.

My first bit of advice is to create a new model, for your own sake as well as your daughter's. There is nothing you can do to stop this thing, but you can alter how quickly you will worsen, with a great deal of hard work, determination and a good support system.

Educate yourself. As you know, this is a rare condition. You need to stay on top of current research. Internaf is a great help. You cannot rely on your doctors alone to do this. Put together a good medical team – doctors who specialize in ataxia, who take you seriously, and take time with you.

I have so many problems, like low back and hip pain, that are secondary to my ataxia. My neurologist works well with my orthopedic surgeon as well as with a pain management specialist.

I have given up on my vision. I now wear a contact lens in my right eye to correct myopia. I have learned to "turn one eye off" at a time. I use my left eye for reading and my right one for distance vision. I have also managed to get used to the double vision. It's amazing what you can learn to live with when you have to. The eyesight problems are what forced me to give up driving two years ago.

I saw all of this coming and I trained to teach via the internet. I am on Social Security/Disability, so I only teach enough to stay under their $740 a month maximum. These days, I commute from my bedroom to the kitchen for coffee and back down the hall to my office. I thought it would be a more difficult transition than it was, but there's a lot to be said about working in your pajamas!

DH: If you are not taking high doses of antioxidant vitamins, discuss this with your doctor right away. Also, you should be taking a good multivitamin. Ataxia saps your strength. Good nutrition is critical and will become even more so as your ataxia progresses.

I place a very high value on fitness, and have done so since my diagnosis in 1989. If you do not have an exercise regimen, you need to think about developing one. I bike on a three-wheeled recumbent, resistance train (Bowflex at home), practice yoga, swim and participate in aqua aerobics (the pool is great – no balance required). I cannot emphasize this enough. You will walk longer and better if you're fit, and fitness is crucial to remaining as independent as possible as your symptoms increase.

I do not need help getting out of bed, transferring from my wheelchair to the toilet, or performing other intimate tasks that I am sure you do not want to think about. It is far easier to stay in shape than it is to get in shape, especially when you are at the stage of ataxia that I am.

It is very normal to want to figure out what to expect; but try not to expect too much. If you anticipate that something should happen within a certain time frame, it very well might. Your positive or negative beliefs will drive you. So start being purposeful about staying strong...even as you know what SCA6 is likely to do both now and in the future.

You have every reason to hope that a treatment will be available to you, but do not plan on it. Do not sit and wait to be rescued from your disease. Be proactive with good nutrition, fitness, and faith as if there will never be a cure. If there is, great. But if not, you'll be ready for that too.

You didn't mention headaches. Do you get them?

I know a lot of people with ataxia that are very uncomfortable with the idea of their using mobility aids (cane, walker, wheelchair). While I respect everyone's individual pace in coming to grips with certain realities of ataxia, I see this as denial, and a form of misplaced vanity. I know folks who would rather stagger like a drunk, hanging on to others, rather than use a mobility aid.

I remember being embarrassed by my father (yes, he was one of those), and I swore my thus-far-unaffected son, who chooses not to have a blood test done right now, would never feel that way about me. I thought that buying my first walker, and then subsequently my first wheelchair, would be some tough moments. Instead, I found them to be instances of true liberation.

Friends: My list of friends is probably a longer one now than it was as a kid, before my FA was visible. I don't go out as often, partly due to the transportation hassles and partly due to issues with fatigue; but a lot has to do with my being a busy mom. I talk daily with friends online, and feel much closer to them now that I am not uncomfortable about the physical problems I have.

Family: I share a similar situation with **SM**, as I also have a younger sister with FA. I think my having ataxia definitely makes my husband and kids and me a more tightly knit unit. Of course, it's kind of a given, when I can't close the bathroom door behind me, or when I consider how often my kids are in my lap, or when my husband is helping me into the shower. As far as our emotional dynamic, we are still pretty close, but I chalk that up more to our personalities than the presence of ataxia.

This is an appropriate conversation for me right now, because tonight I am going out with girlfriends for a much-needed mom's night out. YAY!

Birdsong's Family Members
with
Ataxia & Other Diseases

Walter James Birdsong (Grandfather)
(1-16-1907/11-18-1969)

R.C. Birdsong* (Father)
(4-12-1923/11-28-2000)

Patricia Birdsong Hamilton*
(6-8-1952)

Jimmy Perkins* (Brother)
(3-4-45/5-10-1996)
Died of heart disease

Dillard Birdsong* (Uncle)
(1-28-1936/9-29-2001)

Vanessa Birdsong Booker* (Cousin)
(8-5-1959)

Gennie Sarah Birdsong Hardy** (Aunt)
(9-29-1939)

* Ataxia
**Parkinson's Disease

Patricia's Ataxia Profile

Patricia Birdsong Hamilton
Parents:

    R.C. Birdsong (4-12-23/11-28-00) Age 77

    Annie Lou (Davis) Birdsong (8-17-27/9-9-98) Age 71

Medical conditions: Father – Hereditary ataxia

                      Mother – Alzheimer's disease

Both parents entered an Atlanta nursing home on October 9, 1995.

Siblings :

Robert C. Birdsong (Majied El Amin) (9-18-46)

Walter Lewis Birdsong   (3-27-48)

Angenell Birdsong Nolton   (12-06-53)

Dexter Seymour Birdsong   (11-15-61)

Eric Bernard Birdsong   (3-26-66)

Derrick Lanard Birdsong   (3-26-66)

Jimmy Perkins   (3-4-45/5-10-96)

                            Age 51

Paternal Grandfather:

Walter James Birdsong   Age 62

Patricia's Life Events:

January 1979 – Married

October 1980 – Daughter born

July 1983 – Son born

February 1987 – Diagnosed with ataxia (age 34)

August 1991 – Applied for medical disability from IBM (workplace)

October 7, 1991 – Approved for medical disability (MD)

October 15, 1991 – Left IBM on MD

September 1992 – Applied for Social Security Disability

October 1992 – Denied Social Security Disability

November 1992 – Appealed Social Security
Administration decision

April 1993 – Awarded Social Security retroactive to April 1992

2005 – Coughing and swallowing difficulties

June 2006 – Head and hands tremor

November 27, 2006 – Exam by Dr. George Wilmot,
ataxia specialist

January 16, 2007 – Swallowing test

March 2, 2007 – Take blood test for SCA2 per Dr. Wilmot

Therapy received:

Physical

April 1991 to September 1991 – Burke Rehabilitation

May 2006 to October 2006 – HealthSouth

April 2007 to May 2007 – Gentiva Home Care

Speech

April 1991 to April 1992 – Burke Rehabilitation

July 1995 to November 1995 – Coral
Springs Speech & Language Center

Occupational

August 1991 to October 1991 – Burke Rehabilitation

Education:

Samuel Howard Archer High School – September 1965 to June 1970

Spelman College (Atlanta, GA) – September 1970 to June 1974, Bachelor of Arts, Economics

Atlanta University (Atlanta, GA) – June 1975, Master's of Business Administration, Finance

Key Websites

National Ataxia Foundation (NAF)

www.ataxia.org

email: naf@ataxia.org

2600 Fernbrook Lane, Suite 119

Minneapolis, MN 55447-4752

Phone: (763) 553-0020

Fax: (763) 553-0167

Subscribe to newsletter *Generations*, published 3 to 4 times a year

International Network of Ataxia Friends (Internaf)

www.internaf.org

www.groups.yahoo.com/group/internaf

email: internaf@yahoogroups.com

michel.beaudet@videotron.ca

www.pages.infinit.net/macmike

subscribe: internaf-subscribe@ yahoogroups.com

A very good source of information, it is an online support group which welcomes both members, and family or friends whose loved one has ataxia. Participants are from all over the world.

Late Onset of Friedrich's Ataxia (LOFRDA)
www.onelist.com/community/LOFRDA
www.groups.yahoo.com/group/LOFRDA

Friedrich's Ataxia Parents Group (FAPG)
Email Sue Kittel: fapginfo@fortnet.org

Olivopontocerebellar Atrophy (OPCA) Website
www.alyshia.com/opca

Episodic ataxia
www.hometown.aol.com/mark24609/ataxia/index.html

Machado-Joseph Disease (MJD)
www.ninds.nih.gov/disorders/machado_joseph/detail_
machado_joseph.html

Ataxia Telangiectasia
www.ninds.nih.gov/disorders/a_t/a-t.html

Special Needs Project
www.specialneeds.com

Broward County Florida Ataxia Support Group
(BCFASG)
www.hometown.aol.com/pathamilto/myhomepage/
photo.html

Living with Spinocerebellar Ataxia
www.hometown.aol.com/Pathamilto/myhomepage/
profile.html
email Pat B. Hamilton: addressPathamilto@aol.com

or AtaxiaBooks@aol.com

Life with ataxia (ataxia books and booklets)
www.livingwithataxia.com
email: AtaxiaBooks@livingwithataxia.com

Spinocerebellar ataxia 3
www.home.pacbell.net/fernande/sca3.html

Books, etc.
www.hometown.aol.com/pathamilto/myhomepage/
sale.html

About me! (Spinocerebellar ataxia)
www.home.cfl.rr.com/suttonbeach/aboutme.html

National Organization for Rare Disorders (NORD)
www.rarediseases.org
email: orphan@rarediseases.org

55 Kenosia Ave., PO Box 1968

Danbury, CT 06813-1968

Phone: (203) 744-0100 Toll-free (800) 999-6673 TDD

(203) 797-9590

Fax: (203) 798-2291

This organization is unable to open unexpected email attachments. If you must send one with your email, notify NORD first. If you have questions related to providing care or accessing services for someone with a rare disease, email RN@rarediseases.org. If you have a question related to genetic testing or the inheritance patterns of diseases, email genetic_counselor@rarediseases.org.

Links to mobility and other aids:
    Wheelchair: www.wheelchairnet.org
    Walking stick: www.internaf.org/ataxia/sticks.html
    Life Insurance: www.specialife.com/index.html
    Dynamic Living: www.dynamic-living.com/superpole

Made in the USA